The QUIZ Went Fizz!

Written by Jeanne Willis
Illustrated by Sandra Aguilar

Zebra is in the quiz.
Fox is in the quiz.

I will win!
He will not!

Zip it, Zebra!

3

4

Zebra is quick to buzz.

Will a can of pop go fizz?

3

3

Buzz! Buzz! Buzz!

Me! Me! Yes, a can of pop will go fizz!

Fox wins! Zebra did not buzz.

I had a go. But my buzz went fizz.

My quiz is wet!

Mop Mop